NEW ENGLAND CULTURE & MINISTRY DYNAMICS

*Where You Serve
Makes a Difference
in How You Serve*

I0101521

J. David Jackson

Screven and Allen Publishing

NEW ENGLAND CULTURE
& MINISTRY DYNAMICS

"What New England is, is a state of mind, a place where dry humor and perpetual disappointment blend to produce an ironic pessimism that folks from away find most perplexing."
— Willem Lange, author of "A Yankee Notebook" weekly column

"New Englanders began the Revolution not to institute reforms and changes in the order of things, but to save the institutions and customs that already had become old and venerable with them; and were new only to a few stupid Englishmen a hundred and fifty years behind the times."
— Edward Pearson Pressey, History of Montague: A Typical Puritan Town

"Withstanding the cold develops vigor for the relaxing days of spring and summer. Besides, in this matter as in many others, it is evident that nature abhors a quitter."
— Arthur C. Crandall, New England Joke Lore: The Tonic of Yankee Humor

"Explaining the Jews in a Catholic school when you're Irish is like having to explain your country's foreign policy while on a vacation in France. You don't know what you're talking about and no matter what you say, they're not going to like it anyway."
— John William Tuohy, No Time to Say Goodbye: Memoirs of a Life in Foster Care

"To the rest of the country,
New England has always stood
in much the same relation as
England has to America –
that of spiritual homeland and mother country."
-- B.A. Botkin, author of A Treasury of New England Folklore

"What is required is sight and
insight -- then you might
add one more: excite."
--Robert Frost, Poet (1874-1963)

Other Publications by the Author

PlantLIFE: Principles and Practices in Church Planting (2008)

Planted: Starting Well, Growing Strong (2012)

ReNEW: Traveling the Forgotten Path (2017)

Elevate! Church Planting for Years 3-7, Learner edition (2018)

PREFACE

I came to New England for the first time in the summer of 1977. I was immediately and irrevocably captured by the intoxicating mix of history, culture, beauty, passion, and mystique that make this region different from anywhere else. With exceptions, I've lived here most of my adult life. Two of my children were born here. My family even traces its heritage back to William Brewster and the Mayflower.

But I didn't grow up here. My formative and educational years were spent, like most of you reading this book, a thousand miles away, in another distant and different region of the country. All I knew of New England before that fateful summer in 1977 was found in history books or on annual pictorial calendars.

What I found here was starkly different from what I'd known in other parts of America. At first I was curious. Then, I was resistant. But gradually, New England won me over. So much so that I now revel in the life and experiences I share in this most precious of places.

To be sure, I may never be accepted as a native by those who have lived here for generations (my only saving grace in my "Mayflower card"). But I have learned to value and appreciate New England, to love it and its people for the uniqueness this region represents. And I am all the better for it.

This book is a feeble attempt to help newcomers and visitors, including mission teams, to appreciate and understand the differences that make this region "New England." And to that end, it is offered, to help you in your pursuit of ways to minister and share the Gospel effectively among these precious people. May God use it to His glory and honor.

J. David Jackson
June 11, 2018

TABLE OF CONTENTS

FENWAY PARK
A Microcosm of New England

On May 14, 1999, the owners of Fenway Park in Boston, the baseball stadium that sits beyond Kenmore Square at the intersection of Brookline Avenue and Jersey Street (formerly Yawkey Way), proposed to build a new baseball park. They proposed to replace the old, historic stadium with "New Fenway," a state of the art facility, with all the newest and best creature comforts the sports and recreational world had to offer. They even offered to save a part of old Fenway, as a playground for the community where children would have the opportunity to run from first base to second base, just as a century of baseball players had done previously.

You would have thought a nuclear weapon had been unleashed on the residents of Boston proper, and on New England at large. "Your concerns are our concerns," CEO John Harrington said, to the residents of the city. But residents, local business leaders, and fans, reacted with a "nostalgic melancholy that a legendary institution would be irreparably altered and fears that mom-and-pop shops would be crowded out." Another opponent said, "It's taking them out of their context and making them a tourist attraction." One neighborhood resident worried that the need for extra land for the new stadium might kick him off his property and require him to relocate to a less lucrative area. The team even acknowledged that it has not yet worked out a full scheme to cope with parking and traffic issues -- a point that activists said would have been crucial to making the stadium proposal work for the tight-knit community.

Red Sox management had hoped they could win support in a city where civic activism is known to delay or even torpedo projects. And to be fair, there were many who even liked the new proposal---but for typical New England reasons. `They're doing the right thing and doing a good job of it. They're making it like the old one so you'll have some of the same feel," he said. ``It's good for the team." "The proposal is very clever in its efforts to replicate the existing park and preserve its cultural heritage."

Ultimately, *Save Fenway Park*, a prominent community group had an architect draw up a counter proposal to renovate, rather than rebuild, Fenway. The renovation strategy won the day. One opinion summed up the sentiment: "I love this old park. It's got that small, cozy feeling." Fenway was preserved, renovated, and remains to this day, a symbolic center of what it takes to make New England special.

For those who have lived here for generations, the reasons are obvious. Fenway is more than just a place on the National Historic Registry. It is more than just an institution. It is a familiar friend, one that has always been there, through thick and thin. It is a home away from home for many, full of generational memories and experiences. Fenway is woven into the fabric of New England life in ways so intricate and complex that few outside of New England can understand.

But if you take a minute to look back through the comments made by residents, you'll begin to understand. Values gush through the comments, and the norms of life here are exceedingly evident.

Old
Past
Tradition
Historic
Small
Intimate

Add to these the additional values of:

Summer
Urbane
Participatory
Individual, yet communal
Religious (yes, baseball is a religion here, much like football in the SEC)
And the distain of the dreaded New York Yankees

Suddenly, you begin to understand New England in a new light. You realize it is different. You sense its uniqueness.

You appreciate its distinction. And hopefully, like a wise cross-cultural missionary who has entered an unknown land, you can connect with its values.

Yes, there is little in New England more revered, more treasured than historic Fenway Park, the oldest baseball park in the United States (1912). For it is far more than just a baseball field. It represents what makes New England so special, so proud.

You're invited to turn the page, and look a little closer at New England culture. Together with the Holy Spirit leading, we can learn how to build bridges to the inhabitants with the Gospel of Jesus Christ.

NEW ENGLAND CULTURE
& MINISTRY DYNAMICS

To be sure, we are all products of our time and place in history. Much has been written in past years about the differences in perception and values among the generations that make up the people of this land. Writers, like Gary McIntosh (*Three Generations*), have shown the significant impact that the events of a generational lifetime have upon all its members. On the other hand, relatively few writers have attempted to demonstrate the same kind of significant impact that the geography of a people have upon their values. In this book we shall attempt to do just that.

New England (defined as the states of Maine, New Hampshire, Vermont, Massachusetts, Rhode Island, and Connecticut), with claims to being the oldest "region" in the country (apologies to Virginia), carries significant nuances in its cultural schema that demand contextualization of the Gospel. For decades the leader and pacesetter for Americans in economic, political and social issues, New England in the last seventy-five years has settled into an on-going tension between its love for the past and its claims to the future. At the center of the Industrial Revolution that moved America to world prominence, it hesitated over movement into the digital era. To be sure, Boston, and most notably the universities and institutes of the metropolitan area, have attempted to continue to lead the way. Most of New England, though, has followed at a much more random pace, allowing the Pacific Rim arguably to leave them in the dust. Many urban New Englanders have misgivings about the hesitancy that has so dramatically reduced the region in some regards to an also-ran. "If only we could try again, we would do things differently," is their slogan.

Religion, though, is different. The leader in bringing religious movements to America, New England has also produced most of the significant revival and awakenings in this country's short history. Thus, while other parts of this land are experimenting with new forms for Christianity, and new religions in general, New Englanders live in the paradox of its history---old forms are good forms while no form leads to new forms. In other words, most New Englanders live with a post-Christian mindset, so new spiritual forms are found to satisfy a growing spiritual hunger throughout the region. On the other hand, for New England Christians, the new paradigms that are transforming Christianity across America have, for the most part, made little significant impact here.

For many the old forms are good enough, and always will be. So what is it that makes New England unique, different from all other parts of the United States, in its values and norms? And how do these things contribute to the way the church goes about being the church here?

At least five sets of values can be found in New England, divisible based upon their impact upon the people of the area. The historical values deal with the rich and storied past found in this region, and significantly color all other beliefs held today. The geographical values were among the first assessed and assimilated in this land by our forefathers here. The cultural values developed over time, particularly among those who helped shape the New England experience for so many. The economic values were born out of the crucible of human experience here among the settlers, and passed down to their descendants. The religious values derive from the Puritan influence and its strong teachings on discipline in lifestyle (most often interpreted today as "public" lifestyle).

1
THE KEY HISTORICAL VALUES
(Years)

History is defined as the significant accumulated impact of events over time. The last two words, "over time," suggest the import of history on a region that now dates its history to almost 400 years (Plymouth will celebrate in 2020.). Consequently, the people of this area value what is old more than what is new. Why? Often it is because what is old is tried and true; because it has withstood the test of time. The past, as well, becomes a barometer for present activity and future plans. This is not only because New England has so much of it (the past, that is), but also because the past has been so glorious and revered, not just here but throughout America. The current American scenario cannot be said to look to New England to take the lead in national affairs, as it did in previous days. European (Old World) influence is predominant in this region, too, far more than that of Central America, Asia, Africa, or the Caribbean. A quick check of immigration numbers over the past 150 years will demonstrate the continuing impact that the values and mindset of Europe have on many who live here.

Two notable values yet unmentioned but among the most significant, not just historically but *in toto*, are intellectualism and tradition. The highly educated populace of New England (higher than that of any other region), coupled with the fact that there are more schools of higher education here than anywhere else (237 in New England, 70 in Boston alone), suggests that the region has come to exalt the intellect, often to the exclusion of other forms of expression. For example, the emotionalism of some religious expressions or ethnic peoples are disparaged as the acts of "ignorant rednecks." Add to this value the rich history of starting the storied Ivy League schools (and their equivalents) in the centuries gone by, and intellectualism becomes almost a religion to some people.

Tradition, on the other hand, is born out of experience, and as such, New Englanders again have more than any other

Americans. It has been defined as the tried and true "chains of habits" forged over time. Pioneers advanced these early customs and as they successfully accomplished their purposes and the people grew familiar with them, the customs became tradition. Tradition by its very nature speaks of experience and history bound together in a "working" fashion. So strong is this value in New England life that virtually every new and/or different idea is measured by what has been done before. Many discount the effectiveness of any such change before it even has been heard. At the very least New Englanders are reluctant to embrace anything that challenges tradition unless it can be shown to (a) enhance their economic welfare, or (b) improve their quality of life. Even then, they are reluctant to part from the ways of the past. To some, especially in the older generations, it is akin to cultural treason.

Summary: New England values what is old, what is past, what is European (Old World), what is intellectual, and what has been bathed in tradition.

Implications for Ministry: Ministers and churches must be careful not to throw out "the baby with the bath water." While many in America are discarding the trappings of tradition, New England ministers would do well to build upon it and enhance it wherever possible. New ministries should be introduced as chances to establish new traditions.

Second, recognize that for many people in the area, "new" does not necessarily mean better. Be able to explain why something new is needed, if it is, or learn to value what may be old, instead.

Third, a more cognitive, intellectual approach in witnessing and in worship will be more successful to many native New Englanders. While younger generations value personal experience and emotion more, even they will rarely defy their mental hertiage. However, when experiential or emotional elements are introduced to the congregation, a good way to gain their acceptance is to announce it as a "trial" or "experiment."

Finally, understand the European cultural elements in your community. While New England is more monolithic in culture than most, the varying European influences and values will help any minister to understand his community better and to unlock doors of ministry to its people.

2
THE KEY GEOGRAPHICAL VALUES
(Area)

For the early settlers who had no conception of America as a future nation stretching from ocean to ocean, few would have thought that the region of New England that had come to be their home would be so small. But compared to the other regions in our country it is decidedly smaller. Natural barriers (like rivers and mountains) accounted for much of this originally. Rather quickly though, New Englanders embraced the petite size of their region. So much so, in fact, that "small town living" became the standard characterization for the villages of this northeastern area. Short distances in travel, condensed communities dotting the landscape, and a place where everybody seemed to (at least they thought) know everybody, created a level of intimacy among the natives that was highly valued. It also made New Englanders suspicious of "outside" (beyond New England) influences that suggested bigger was inevitably better. The intimacy within the environment fostered a sense of community that was, and still is, prized by the townspeople throughout the region. With town fairs and annual celebrations, the spirit of community is perennially rekindled among the people. With it comes a jealous pride for the region itself that ties New Englanders closer to one another than the people in other parts of this land. Many families in fact would never even consider leaving this region of the country. It is home to them in more ways than one.

An interesting addition to these geographical values is the observation that New England in many ways has a closer kinship with England (Great Britain) than with the rest of the United States. Some British immigrants have even suggested that the region reminds them more of the place of their birth than where they now live in this country (U. K. Pastors would be included in this group). Perhaps it is because New England existed as a part of England for one hundred and fifty years before the United States was born. Since America is less than two hundred and fifty years old, it is easy to see how England

NEW ENGLAND CULTURE

could impact it so significantly.

Summary: New England values what is small (like itself), a sense of community more intimate than most, and takes strong jealous pride in its region and its English roots.

Implications for Ministry: There are some significant insights for ministers here. First, since the largest non-Catholic church in New England is only about 3,500 people (very small by national standards), think about how you can grow your church and still maximize the value of being small. Multisite locations and multiple services are two possible ways this can be done. Be careful not to emphasize that something is better just because it is bigger.

Second, enhance fellowship and the intimacy it can bring. Carry it into all areas of church life, from worship to polity to outreach—not just over a cup of coffee or a meal. It could become one of your church's greatest strengths.

Finally, keep an ear to our Christian ministers across the sea in Great Britain and learn from them, not just from American models and ministers. British ministers are constantly reminding New Englanders that they have been where we now are (about a generation ago, they say), and that things are improving in Britain in recent years. They can tell you why and how to share this reality in a humanist, post-Christian world.

3
THE KEY CULTURAL VALUES
(Influence)

The impact of New England upon the culture of the United States is felt in many ways. The following three values are among the most significant ways in which New England is constantly influencing the nation.

The emphasis upon quality over quantity is almost a natural corollary to the value of smallness mentioned above. In defiance of other regions that promote "more" as the measure of success (California, Texas, et al.), New England has responded with "better is best." This is evident in the continual tension that exists between New York City and Boston. Each representative of their respective regions, they stand poles apart on this issue. To New Englanders, New York City represents the worst case scenario in valuing numbers above all else. Higher crowds, higher crime, higher complexity as New Englanders see it, do not equal a better life. On the contrary, while New York City boasts it has everything at its disposal as "a city that never sleeps," Boston suggests that it has everything that's worth having, and wastes its time on nothing else. For example, the quality schools and quality hospitals in their area are virtually unparalleled in the world.

A second cultural value New Englanders have bequeathed to America is its rugged individualism. Born in the wild of the colonial days, it continues to be fueled by its town meetings where every voice is worth hearing. The fierce independent spirit that helped give birth to a nation still resides in the heart of most New Englanders. That emphasis on individualism has led to a "my way is always okay" mentality among many in the current generation that doesn't want to be told what to be or do.

The third cultural value that has significantly impacted the nation is tolerance. Paralleling the value of individualism, this value suggests that while my way may be best for me, you have the right to choose your own way, and it can be just as "right"—for you, that is. This value has germinated in the movement toward "political correctness;" which has some of its seeds on the academic campuses in the region. Tolerance has become a value of which most residents in New England now boast significantly as the result of an "enlightened" people, in contradistinction to what they perceive in other regions of the country, especially in the South.

Summary: Culturally, New Englanders have embraced and espoused the values of quality, individualism, and tolerance in strong and forceful ways to the rest of the country.

Implications for Ministry: Quality becomes a benchmark for most New Englanders in ministry, especially visitors to your church. Be sure to have the best your church can offer in worship and ministry. Nowhere is this more significant than in the worship hour and with children's ministries. Remember also not to maximize quantity above quality in ministry. While both are important, to most New Englanders quality always comes first.

Tolerance is going to be one of the greatest continuing challenges for the evangelical church of the twenty-first century in New England. The charges of elitism and exclusivity must be overcome in action. The exclusive claims of the Gospel should not be compromised; rather they must be paralleled by the inclusive love of Christ.

Individualism gives ministers a great chance to equip believers according to their spiritual gifts, their passions in ministry, and their skill and maturity levels. Congregational polity that highlights this value will be seen as more indigenous to the region, as well.

4
THE KEY ECONOMIC VALUES
(Material Impact)

From the Pilgrims in the early years forward into the early decades of the twenty-first century, the region of New England has not been an easy one to tame. The harsh winters and the difficulties in establishing "cash crops" here led to the development of a differing mentality in regards to the economy. What has transpired since has only heightened the emphasis placed upon it. As a farming people in the early years, the value of perseverance was quickly acknowledged. This was particularly recognized as important due to the rocky soil and the long winter months. Learning how to wait and how to succeed through endurance became habits sewn into the very fabric of the people of this region.

In addition, the limited resources quickly at their disposal taught New Englanders the value of being frugal. Coupled with the Puritan ethic that we shall discuss shortly, the natives of the area (for the most part) learned to resist opulence and luxury, and long for the plain and simple life. While "pockets" of extravagance can surely be found, they would be the exception to the rule in this part of the country. New Englanders would be more likely to "do without" and hold on to their possessions and money for "a rainy day."

New Englanders also over time have come to value what is indigenous and "home grown" as opposed to the imported goods and services received, even from other regions of the country. Perhaps this is because they understand the toil and endurance of their fellow New Englanders; perhaps it is because they truly feel no one else apart from the region can appreciate their tastes and needs as well as they themselves can. Regardless, it is a chronicled "fact" that businesses that survive in New England either are indigenous to the area or are willing to take major losses in the early years to become established in the region. Franchise stores and restaurants are one good example of where this value can be clearly seen.

Summary: The people of this region have learned the values of perseverance and frugality. They prefer what is indigenous to New England over almost anything "imported" from beyond its borders.

Implications for Ministry: Churches would do best to find ministers from within New England itself. That being said, ministers that come to New England from other regions should acclimate themselves to the region as quickly and comprehensively as possible. In addition, they should make a commitment to be in the work of ministry here "for the long haul." Change will not happen fast in two-hundred year old churches, and new churches will not flourish quickly. It takes an enduring, persevering mindset. For those from outside the area looking for new places to start work, the best indicator of receptivity will be found in towns and cities that are open to outside influences, such as franchise stores and restaurants. In these locations, at least, governing officials are open to the influence and impact of life beyond New England.

Frugality will be an issue in budgeting and financing the work of any church. The suggestion here is to get permission as early as you can through good reasoning and communication. Tight-fisted financial officers make adding ministries harder at inopportune moments. Teach the congregation what God expects and model good stewardship yourself.

5
THE KEY RELIGIOUS VALUES
(Puritan)

The lifestyle of New Englanders has been significantly influenced by their forefathers of the Massachusetts Bay Colony, the Puritans (sometimes referred to as "America's Pharisees"). These Reformed theologians took a very stern view of life and its practices, and declared extremely tight boundaries in how one was to live. While most of the theological values of the Puritans were discarded decades ago, the pervasive influence of their decrees is widely and strongly felt even to this day among the people of the region. Among the ways they impact the life of the region are the following six things.

The "culture of discomfort" is a phrase coined by *Yankee Magazine* to express the expectation of formality experienced in many New England circles to this day. While high collars and shoe length dresses may not be the fashion of the day, a sense of discomfort in the way one dresses and feels is the assumed norm in these parts of the country. There are probably many reasons for it, from respect for those who have gone before to the inclement weather. Still New Englanders boast in their ability (and choose) to live through the discomforts.

Many in the region couple this with an austerity and sternness that gives one the feeling that all of life is to be met with seriousness. The Puritans in all likelihood drove this home in their generation by emphasizing the significance of reverence and respect. The lack of amusement and fun experienced then often makes it hard for their descendants to feel that it is acceptable to enjoy "light" moments and warm, affectionate responses.

Guilt was a natural consequence for most who lived in an era that condemned so much as "of the devil." The severity of the punishments and the frequency of the claims did much to heighten the sense of guilt for many who lived here during that day. Some no doubt even felt guilty when they had done nothing wrong, but simply because they knew they were being watched (a kind of seventeenth century "Big Brother"), and thought out of their ignorance they might be charged with misbehavior of some sort. These feelings were transferred to children and grandchildren until today, when many New Englanders still avoid the church and its influence simply because of the guilt they feel. (Some of this keeps people away in all parts of the world, to be sure; here we are talking about an exaggerated guilt that may or may not be founded in sin.)

The above suggests a progression in attitude that might lead the inhabitants to be pessimistic about the affairs and course of life. Factor in the harsh conditions of climate and economy, and pessimism becomes the norm for New Englanders. The open unhappiness, even cynicism, with the "way things are" is standard fare in the news media of the region, as writers decry the factors and conditions (specifically politicians and athletic teams) that make their lives so miserable. Little hope is ever held out that the future will be any different than the past.

New Englanders have also learned, probably from their Puritan ancestors, to be frank and direct in their words and actions. They rarely use "flowery" words or "beat around the bush." Such embellishment or subtlety is seen as pretense or dishonesty, and an attempt to hide the truth. In contrast, within the South a politeness that often masks the truth for the sake of not taking offense or embarrassing someone, especially with those who don't know you closely, is assumed and expected in public. In New England, such a politeness would be considered "lying" and one's motives would come under subsequent attack.

As a result of the five characteristics listed above, New Englanders seem outwardly prudish about lifestyle issues, especially of sexuality. While inwardly tolerant and politically liberal for the most part, their public behavior exhibits strong signs of a conservative bent. They are rarely unruly or blatant about their vices. In fact, they of all the regions in the country still "hide" pornography behind the counters of convenience stores, and fight publicly to oppose the influence of "adult" businesses in their communities. Their argument: it violates community standards, something to be considered when one studies the culture of any people.

Summary: New Englanders carry much of the baggage of their Puritan ancestors that affects their behavior, making them value discomfort, austerity, directness, and an outwardly conservative community lifestyle. It also makes a sense of guilt and pessimism about life the norm among its people.

Implications for Ministry: There are many implications for ministry in this section. For example, giving people permission to be casual in dress or merry in attitude may be offered, but without the ability to release them from the power of the guilt they will feel about even this, it will not happen for many. Teaching them a proper perspective on guilt is crucial for these values and norms to be rectified. Add to this the reality that optimism and joy are more caught than taught and one will sense the importance that example can make. Make sure that your optimism is well-grounded, and is not confused with naïveté. Otherwise, many will "write you off" before you are seen or heard.

Finally, learn to appreciate the frank, direct approach. Don't take it personally. (For many Southerners this may be hard.) Learn to appreciate the value of knowing where your people are "at" as they speak their minds, instead of holding thoughts to themselves. Ministry bottlenecks that are relational in nature are often streamlined or eliminated in this way.

6
OTHER RELIGIOUS NORMS

While the Puritan mindset and religion would dominate the behavioral aspects (ethics) of the people in New England, the outward forms of religion have changed over the years. Three norms have become notable within the region.

First, within the religious community there has been a rigid grip on Christian orthodoxy. Variants have historically been treated severely and culturally such parishioners have been ostracized. From within, doctrinal "purity" was to be maintained at all costs. Add to this belief the emphases already noted on tradition and indigeneity, and one begins to understand why religious fringe groups or cults rarely prosper in this area. Those that do are usually both emphasize intellectualism and indigeneity, as with Christian Science or Unitarian-Universalists, and are persevering in their ministry, overcoming obstacles through time and determination.

Second, Roman Catholicism has become the "rule," not the exception, in religious practice within New England. This is a significant historical and cultural phenomenon, since Catholics were banned in the early days and did not appear "in masse" until just over a hundred and thirty years ago (around 1880). This mostly has to do with the import of European immigration to this country, especially from Ireland and Italy, before and after the turn of the last century. Regardless, its influence is pervasive and must be acknowledged.

Outside the traditional religious community in the region, the wide majority of inhabitants would be secularists, living in a postmodern world. The norm would be a form of humanism that emphasized the value and goodness of humanity, the supremacy of science and the intellect, and decries (not out loud, you understand) religion as a form of manipulation, playing on the fears of the people. These people would see religion in general, and Christianity in particular, as yesterday's news and irrelevant, from a paternalistic, intolerant era with its unwanted claims upon one's life. The primary response to the pleas of Christ would be apathy and indifference, if not downright hostility.

Summary: New Englanders have come to see the religious landscape in the region change over the years until the non-religious secular humanists predominate. Within the religious community Roman Catholics are a wide majority. Anything unorthodox in religious belief or practice will have great difficulty surviving here, unless it is born from within the culture itself.

Implications for Ministry: Most of what the church confronts here will be secular humanists in a postmodern mindset. Learn what you can about it. (An excellent overview resource is *SoulTsunami* by Leonard Sweet.) Don't downplay their sources of authority, like reason or science. Challenge their underpinings and assumptions, instead. Take apologetic approaches to the Scripture seriously and learn to use them. Be determined to make every sermon and Bible study emphasize the practical relevance the Word of God has to life.

Don't spend as much time with traditional cult awareness as in other areas of the country. Do understand the mind cults of the area (they combine with the secular humanism mentioned above). Do everything you can to understand and "appreciate" what Roman Catholicism (European, not Latin) is all about in this part of the country (to many it is more cultural than religious).

7
FINAL NORMS

By nature most New Englanders are suspicious of outsiders (from beyond the region). Their history and experience has taught them that outsiders bring different values and agendas to the area, often without the permission or understanding of those who have lived here their whole lives. This suspicion causes New Englanders to question authority (the obvious exception is within the universities, where almost everyone is an outsider), and to be slower to commit to a departure from what they have known in the past.

The indigenous residents also tend to carry a high amount of pent-up anger and dysfunctionality in their dealings with circumstances and relationships in life. For example, the cases of abuse and crimes of passion are extremely high in the area, as are the number of alcoholics, addictions, and individuals involved in support groups of one sort or another. One can only guess as to the reasons why: more generational "baggage" than other areas, the harshness of the weather and the terrain, the busyness of life in a high-pressure society (not all of it has to do with the place where they reside). Still, these things obviously impact the attitudes and behavior of the people as they interact.

Summary: New Englanders are suspicious of outsiders, and have higher degrees of anger and dysfunctional symptoms that are more visible within New England community life than those of most other Americans.

Implications for Ministry: Think about using support groups in your church to minister to the many around you with vice, anger, and functionality problems. If you are an outsider to the region, try to understand the suspicions New Englanders may have. Earn their trust through time and integrity. Surround yourself with indigenous leadership as well and as fast as you can. Give the ministry away to them. It will thrive better in their hands.

So here, in this book we have attempted to focus attention on some of the specific values and norms of significance in the region of New England. In particular, it is an effort to contrast it with other parts of the United States. Better clarification for ministry has been its goal as we seek to bring the Gospel message to the people of the region.

A more extensive chart, showing these values and norms, and including others, as well, may be found on the following page. In the subsequent pages, the reader will find specific applications of these values and norms in ministry within your community, in the context of Boston, and also, beyond.

NEW ENGLAND VALUES AND NORMS
A Study in Contrast

Regional	vs.	National

The Historical Values

Tradition	over	Innovation
Intellect	over	Emotion
Old	over	New
Past	over	Future
Auditory	over	Visual
Liberal Politics	over	Conservative
Old World	over	Third World

The Geographical Values

Small	over	Large
Region	over	Nation
Community	over	City
Big Group (>35)	over	Small Group (<35)
England	over	California
Outdoors	over	Indoors

The Cultural Values

Quality	over	Quantity
Individuality	over	Conformity
Tolerance	over	Elitism
Baseball	over	Basketball

The Economic Values

Perseverance	over	Quick Fix
Indigenous	over	Imported
Blue Collar	over	White Collar
Frugality	over	Luxury

The Religious Values

Discomfort	over	Comfort
Formality	over	Informality
Austere	over	Flamboyant
Guilt	over	Joy
Direct	over	Polite
Conservative Lifestyle	over	Carefree Living
Reserved	over	Open
Pessimism	over	Optimism

Other Norms (including Religious Norms)

Orthodox	over	Unorthodox
Catholic	over	Protestant
Secularism	over	Christianity
Suspicious	over	Trusting
Anger	over	Content
Dysfunctional	over	Functional

BUT! The younger the adult audience, the more like the "national value/norm" they will be.

NOTE: This does not apply to first generation ethnic immigrants or Anglo-Americans who move here from other parts of the USA or Canada, until they have been in New England for multiple generations.

KNOWING YOUR AUDIENCE

When I was growing up in the deep South (Alabama, Tennessee, Louisiana), I "learned" by default that all Americans—at least Anglo-Americans—were essential "the same." Not their jobs, their church, or their sports allegiance. But their values, their norms, and even, I assumed, their lifestyle.

This was certainly never true in America, though the fifties and early sixties may have made it appear that way. At least, this was the way it was portrayed in the media, and especially on television. Aspired ideals were typically portrayed on the screen; not life as it truly was.

At the Christian college I attended I can still, very dramatically, remember the evening I heard a woman with the non-descript name of Mary Smith share that she had lived in the Northeast for several years and never even known you could have a personal relationship with God through Jesus Christ. At the time, this was totally foreign to me, and in fact, overwhelming. How could anyone live in America and not know this reality?!

Over time, with the splintering of America's monolithic society into multiple factions, it has been easy to realize several things. First, I lived in a very sheltered Christian bubble in the South, where our form of religion dominated (maybe consumed is a better word) all aspects of my life. Most of American was not like this, though many from the South might find familiarity with my experience. Second, media shifted from promoting the ideal values to the "real" values, with its myriad varieties of opinions and alternatives. Philosophically, this was a huge shift from a common Judeo-Christian ethic, to a "anything goes" mentality. And third, multiple corporate, societal experiences since the 1960s have dramatically seared into the course of American life for us all. These events and experiences have shaped us differently, and cause us to address the concerns of life in no uniform fashion.

While we are not at liberty in this short book to highlight all of these experiences, it should underscore the reality that we cannot do ministry for our Lord today like it was done in the past. We must be missionaries, exploring and understanding the people and places we serve with the eyes of an outsider, seeking to understand. Understanding can lead to awareness. Awareness leads to appreciation. Appreciation can lead to connection, and that gives opportunity for the Gospel.

We have "sliced" New England culture many ways in the previous pages. I do not intend to revisit those ways here. But I do want to make sure you are aware of an additional nuance you will have to address in the community where you serve.

Every community is unique, and in New England, the residents certainly have no hesitation to let you know. The town next door is not the same (or nearly as good) as their own. This personality, or character, is part of what makes each community different. And for you, the new resident, it presents a challenge, both to understand and to engage.

Then within every city, town, and village you will find two types of people: natives and immigrants. And they see things, and deal with things, in a very different way. The terminology I used may make you think I'm talking about ethnicity, but I am not. Rather, I'm talking about residency. Natives, or "townies," as they are often called here, have lived in your community all their lives, perhaps for generations. Immigrants are transplants, like most of you reading this book, who have moved into a community and seek to make life there.

Natives are typically the insiders. Immigrants, the outsiders.
Natives are typically the gatekeepers. Immigrants, not so much.
Natives are the cultural mavens. Immigrants, the ignorant.
Natives are nuanced and situated. Immigrants are blatant and unsettled.
Natives are in the know. Immigrants are oblivious or wanting to know.
Natives appreciate the heritage. Immigrants disregard its value.
Natives are resistant to change. Immigrants often promote the change.

There are many other differences that could be cited. The point here is to know the one you are. Are you a native or an immigrant?

This is important because you will more easily reach those like yourself, and more likely repel the opposite group, at the same time. It takes a very sensitive, aware leader, to effectively reach both groups—at least from the beginning. Over time, prayers and efforts to find "persons of peace" (Luke 10:6) will enable you to reach into the other audience, as well. And by that time, many of your church's values and norms (built off of your own values and norms, and those of your leadership team) will be formed.

You will have to adapt like a missionary, or expect those you reach to adapt. If that is your expectation, some will do so effectively, but don't be surprised if some never will. Nor will they want to do so. It may not be who they are.

Now, God can do anything! I realize this. Certainly, if He can talk through a donkey, He can bring people to you who are different in background, values, and heritage. But until He does, think like a missionary, and analyze who you are reaching. Build bridges where you can, and maximize the opportunities to broaden your audience to reach others.

Just know that people are different. And it will take different people to reach them. Who are you trying to reach? If you are an immigrant to New England, then share the Gospel with everyone you can, but realize you will likely have greater impact on other immigrants with the Gospel. And pray that as God leads indigenous people into His forever family, they will be able to reach more natives with the same forever message of hope and eternity.

And if you are a native, do the same, knowing that you have a built-in advantage with the locals in your community, and may have a more difficult time appreciating and valuing what outsiders bring to your locale.

I have reflected many times on my college experience in learning that American culture differs across the country. There are Mary Smiths all around us who need the Gospel. We must not be naïve, or ignorant as we seek to share Jesus with them. The message is clothed in the messenger. Know your audience, and step by step introduce them effectively to Jesus.

"THE HUB OF THE UNIVERSE"

This is the phrase Bostonians use to describe our city. To be sure, it is arrogant, audacious, and overreaching. Yet, it is life as we know it in New England.

The "urban jungle". It's a phrase we're more likely to use to describe the challenging city environment where more and more of our population lives every year. Business, recreation, tourism, education, and family life all converge in the teeming masses that inhabit Boston, and our other cities. The sheer volume of people who live in these places create a unique opportunity for the church in the twenty-first century. In reality, with more than half of the American population now living in the urban world (about the same in the metro Boston area here as this reality is in other parts of the United States), it's more than an opportunity; it's a responsibility. We must take the Gospel to them.

Historically, we have been weak in our efforts to impact the cities. Our strength has been located in the rural and suburban areas. To our credit, we've recognized the sociological changes that led to urban migration and have attempted to embrace the challenge of urban ministry. However, early efforts led to modest, limited impact. Not before the national strategy of the past decade have we really found any modicum of effectiveness. The reason is church planting.

Over the past twenty years of my work in the world of church planting, I've discovered that no two church plants are the same. All of them are unique in special ways, from the planter who serves with God to establish it, to the name that expresses their identity and purpose, to the environment in which they serve. Nowhere are these differences more significant than in Boston and the cities. Planters and churches who understand and incarnate their own uniqueness as God leads them will find greater success. But they must also come to grips with the following seven things to have long, lasting impact on the urban world in which they serve.

The world of complexity. Everybody is busy; it's our modern world. But nowhere is that more evident than in the city. The complex domains of work or school, family, transportation, and recreation (especially for children) create tensions for social networks and congregational life. They all demand our time, and they pull us in different directions. Busyness and complexity go hand in hand, and make the challenge of church more difficult for many to embrace at the most basic, practical level, even if the desire is there. The key for effective church planting is to keep it simple. This offers refuge for fellow strugglers and security in a volatile, changing world.

The must of diversity. The urban landscape is not monochromatic; it is Technicolor. This diversity is seen not simply in race and ethnicity, but also in economics. In fact, the urban environment is more diversified by socio-economics than anything else. This urban caste system creates "haves" and "have nots," based on education, jobs, wealth, and heritage (in New England and the Northeast, at least), in addition to race and ethnicity. Effective church planters know their own neighborhood well, and transcend these differences with the Gospel in effective, practical ways. They welcome diversity and refuse to allow these sociological differences define God's people.

The seduction of variety. The city offers a buffet of options on everything from outdoor activities to means of transportation. While variety has grown everywhere, the options in the city are endless, and are available 24/7. Comparative analysis and consumer thinking are two inevitable results for city dwellers. "How is this option better than that option?" "What's the benefit to me?" These are the questions that run through the minds of many urbanites. Effective church planters refuse to fall prey to the overwhelming cultural push toward unlimited options. They remain focused in their service, relying on the strengths God has given them and the passion He provides to direct them to carve out their initial niche of impact for Him.

The significance of history. There is hardly a city in America more historic and revered for its patriotism than Boston. In many ways, America as a nation started here. Look around and you will see evidence of its import everywhere.

Landmarks, memorials, and historical markers litter the landscape. Any resident who works or serves here is bound to recognize its value. Residents see it as their heritage. While not unique to the cities, heritage is taken more seriously here. Church planters who want to make inroads with the residents will respect their heritage, and find significance in it.

The impact of higher education. The urban arena in Boston is the laboratory for more higher education than just about any setting in America. Harvard, MIT, and 68 other colleges and universities define much of the dynamic of the city. This adds intellectualism and sophistication to just about everything here. Quality, class, and excellence dominate the presentation of information and experience in life, and thus, affects the way the church is both perceived and is effective in addressing the people of the city. Apologetics are important, as is the polish with which information is transmitted.

The deception of tolerance. Urban society has embraced a sophistication that has redefined basic terms for its own benefit over the years. None has been more readily embraced in Boston and the urban world than "tolerance." The word, which used to mean respect, now means to suggest acceptance. Anything less is seen as racist, misogynist, homophobic, and politically incorrect. Evangelical Christians are often stereotypically thrown into these hateful categories by others. The effective urban church planter knows what he believes and with compassion, refuses to veer from it. He overcomes this slander with demonstrations of love and service, and patient perseverance that is here to stay.

The worth of a soul. Brokenness is a real thing in every life and family. Nowhere is that more evident than in the city. The tensions of urban life stress the greatest of believers. Unredeemed souls too often are shattered by the brute force of the dehumanizing, impersonal forces that undermine their worth. Into this brokenness steps the church to bring a message of hope and worth to those who need it most. Into this reality steps the church to bring good news of reconciliation and redemption for broken and separated people. Into this world steps the church to bring love and an eternal message of value to every life. Effective church planters always keep the main thing, the main thing. They are the ultimate optimists, because they know the ability of our eternal God to "make all things new."

These realities are not just in Boston and our cities, to be sure. Perhaps they are simply magnified there, because of the density of people, the exaggeration of emotion, and the desperation of need. But with each of these realities comes the opportunity for us to demonstrate the difference the Gospel makes. Rather, it is a responsibility we MUST embrace, for it is the power of the Gospel of Jesus Christ (Romans 1:16).

BEYOND BOSTON
Reaching the Rest of New England with the Gospel

You don't have to be in New England long before you discover that the people of these fine states are very different from each other. Vermonters are not Mainers and are quick to tell you so, and Mainers are not the same as their Massachusetts ancestors. And all of the states are ready to tell you that they are not like Boston.

Such is the life in this fair region of the country, where six small, but significant states are found. These states carry the influence of national aspirations, economic well-being, and religious heritage on their shoulders. And as some have noted, "As New England goes, so goes the nation."

We find ourselves here, seeking to plant churches with the Gospel, like John Chapman, known to most as "Johnny Appleseed," planted orchards of trees years ago. Outside of Boston, New England sprawls into rich mountain land, gorgeous forests of colorful trees, and unique church-spired landscapes that define a region. Here, we plant the Gospel itself; here we plant hope found in Jesus Christ.

Nationally, we have loudly and visibly declared our commitment to planting churches in prominent urban centers across North America, including Boston. These efforts are making a difference in reaching the cities with the Good News of Jesus. But we cannot abandon the rest of the region. Rather, our efforts are to do "whatever it takes" to impact all six states in rural, town and village, suburban, as well as urban areas. Here beyond Boston, we lean on our local churches to take the lead, and to establish the practices and missional outposts that will demonstrate the love of Christ and His message of salvation. Here we apply ourselves to planting in ways that make a lasting difference in the fabric of New England.

What are the keys to such a strategy outside of the city? What makes the rest of New England unique?

Love/hate relationships. This starts with "the Hub of the Universe," as Boston promotes itself. The remainder of New Englanders outside of Boston acknowledge the importance of Boston in their lives and to this region. Almost half of the fifteen million people in New England live and work in the metro Boston area, so it obviously impacts them economically. In addition, though, Boston impacts their lifestyle in how they spend their time and money, and attempts to add swagger through its attitude to influence their politics, their opinions, their norms and behaviors, as well. It is here that the "hate" side of the relationship comes to play; New Englanders don't like to be told what to do or think...by anyone, including their "big brother," Boston. Even though Boston may be right, the remainder of New England prefers to learn this on its own, rather than being told what how to act. This love/hate relationship extends to other things, too, including government, sports teams, economic engines (like WalMart or McDonald's), and yes, even the church. Church planters have to be credible and patient to earn a hearing with the Gospel.

Urbane Mentality. Though most New Englanders live outside the city, the city still lives within them. They are urban thinkers, and often invade the urban world for entertainment and opportunity. They have chosen to live apart from Boston or other urban centers, where many lived in previous years, out of personal preference. Yet, they carry their mentality, fed by their education and years of city experience, with them. This affects perceptions, and presents sophistication and intellectualism not ordinary in small towns and country settings across America. Here it drives the ability of planters to connect with the residents who live in the places where they serve.

The More Local the Better. "Mom and Pop shops" rule the roost outside of the city. Why? Relationships—local relationships—that often span generations. This has a corollary in government, too. The town governments are more trusted than the state or the federal government. Local is trusted because it's known, because it's "us." Big bureaucracies are met with suspicion and anger, since lives and livelihoods are at stake. Planters make inroads here by establishing autonomous local churches and reaching indigenous people to lead ministry efforts in the community.

Rugged Individualism. Perhaps only the Wild West values the rugged individualism of humanity more than New England. From his thoughts to his focused determination, the ideal of a New Englander thriving against the elements and against the odds has driven the people of this region for centuries. Translated it means this: they don't like to be told what to do; they prefer to find their own way. The challenge motivates them, the success satisfies them. For planters this means harsh weather or adverse obstacles will be met as challenges, not as insurmountable barriers. New Englanders pride themselves on finding a way to make whatever is necessary to happen.

Beat of a Different Drummer. Because of the adversity our forefathers faced here in this region, they taught themselves to innovate. That meant being countercultural in the eyes of society, and even the world. Over time, they set the pace in many ways for our nation because they refused to conform and fit into the status quo. It shaped them into a frank and direct people who stay focused on the task at hand, regardless of public opinion or what others think about it. Church planters discover this out-of-the-box spirit, and the direct communication early in their experience with New Englanders. Unnerving at first, it becomes a welcome addition to the advancement of the Gospel through the efforts of the new church they establish.

"Summer people." This term is used of many New Englanders for those not from here. It is a term that originally spoke to the large masses of tourists who came here in the short, idyllic summer months, but has grown to represent those who have different values and desires than New Englanders, and hope to impose them upon the locals. "Summer people" are tolerated with some distain (see love/hate relationships above). Over time—and it will take time—the local people will allow planters and a new church to influence their lives. However, this can take decades or even generations. Planters who are in it to stay will find success as they establish their lives here.

Perseverance. Finally, the value of perseverance is necessary in planting a church outside of the city. Every New

Englander who has ever lived here knows that nothing comes easily or quickly in this region of the country. Crops take time to root in the soil, and the weather changes dramatically from season to season. The one who makes it here is the one who survives, who understands the rhythms of life, who perseveres through the difficulties that come. Relationships take time, too, but they are worth it, for eternity is at stake for precious people who need to know of Jesus' great love for them. On farms and in town hall meetings, the people persevere to make decisions that affect their future. Planters will have to persevere in the same way to plant the Gospel, see it take root, and tend it well, for fruit to result.

Today we are having great success also in planting churches here in New England outside of the metropolitan city areas. Church planters in Maine and Vermont, along with other rural areas, are seeing many churches started and new disciples made as the Gospel is planted. It has taken decades of hard work, and diligent, determined commitment to the call of God, but many have responded. As Robert Frost, the New England poet once said, "What is required is sight and insight -- then you might add one more: excite." God is giving us that excitement for what is happening in New England; could He be calling you to join us?

FOR FURTHER STUDY

Boykin, B. A., editor. **A Treasury of New England Folklore: Stories, Ballads, and Traditions of Yankee Folk**, revised edition. New York: American Legacy Press, 1947, 1965, 1989.

Feintuch, Burt, and Watters, David, editors. **The Encyclopedia of New England.** New Haven: Yale University Press, 2005.

Fischer, David Hackett. **Albion's Seed: Four British Folkways in America.** New York: Oxford Press, 1989.

Garreau, Joel. **The Nine Nations of North America.** Publication location unknown: Avon Books, 1982.

Gill, Donald H., editor. **New England Church Resource Handbook.** Boston: Evangelistic Association of New England, 1980.

Hale, Judson D. **Inside New England.** Peterborough, NH: Bauhan Publishing, 2010.

Mayo, Matthew P. **Bootleggers, Lobstermen & Lumberjacks: Fifty of the Grittiest Moments in the History of Hardscrabble New England.** Guilford, CT: GPP, 2011.

McAdow, Ron. **New England Timeline**. Southborough, MA: Nutshell Press, 1991.

McCord, David. **About Boston: Sight, Sound, Flavor & Inflection.** Boston: Little, Brown and Company, 1948, 1973.

O'Brien, Robert, editor, with Brown, Richard D. **The Encyclopedia of New England.** New York: Facts on File Publications, 1985.

Powers, John. **The Boston Handbook.** North Attleborough, MA: Covered Bridge Press, 1999.

Reinstein, Ted. **New England Notebook: One Reporter, Six States, Uncommon Stories**. Guilford, CT: GPP, 2013.

Sletcher, Michael, editor. **New England: The Greenwood Encyclopedia of American Regional Cultures**. Westport, CT: Greenwood, 2004.

Weston, George F., Jr., updated by Raymond, Charlotte Cecil. **Boston Ways: High, By, and Folk.** Boston: Beacon Press, 1957.

Woodard, Colin**. American Nations: A History of the Eleven Rival Regional Cultures of North America.** New York: Penguin Books, 2012.

Yankee magazine. Dublin, NH: Yankee Publishing Inc., since 1935.

NEW ENGLAND CULTURE